AMAZING SPOT WHAT!

Nick Bryant & Rowan Summers

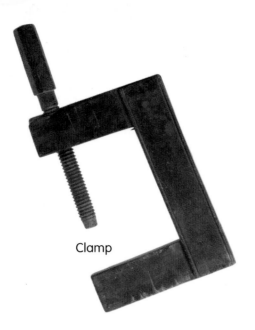

Clamp

Cog

Cat

Abacus

Author: Nick Bryant and Rowan Summers

Joker

Copyright Hinkler Books Pty.Ltd. 2002

Scholastic and Lemon Drop Press and associated logos are trademarks of Scholastic Inc

Published by Lemon Drop Press, an imprint of Scholastic Inc; 557 Broadway; New York, NY 10012

10 9 8 7 6 5 4 3 2 1

ISBN: 0 439 42489 5

Printed and bound in Singapore

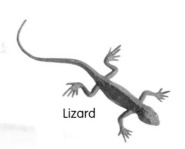

Car

Lizard

Mouse

Balloon

Contents

Knight

Whistle

Vice

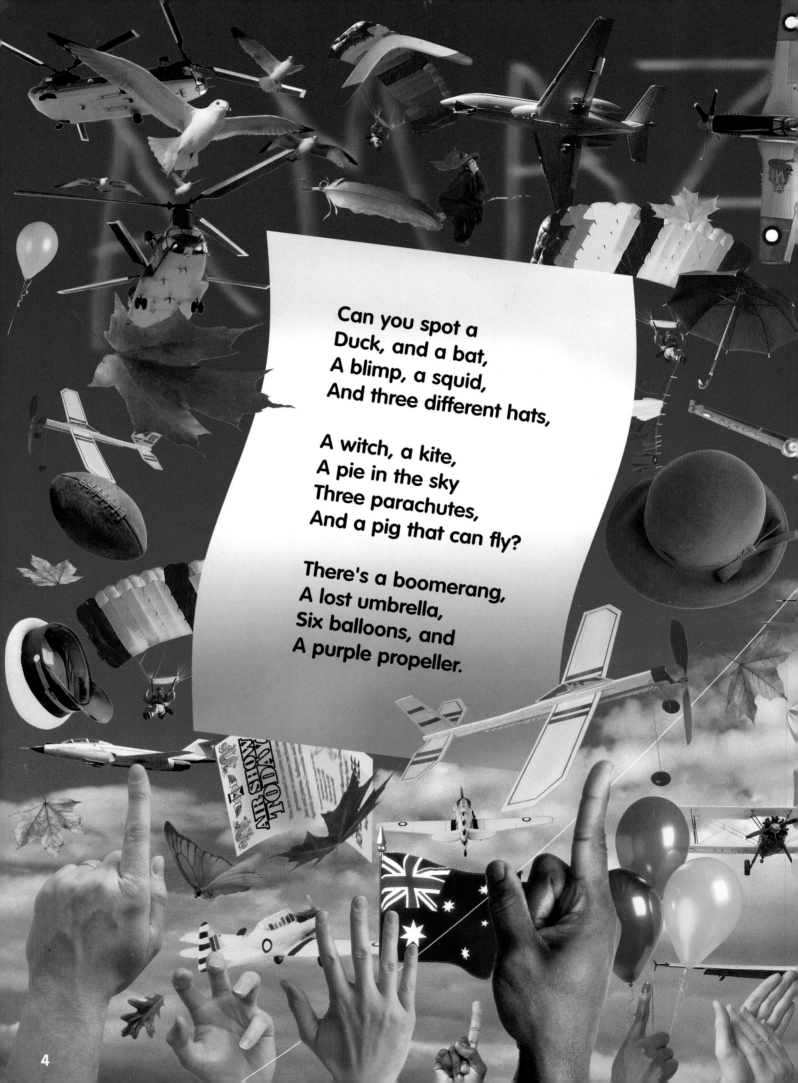

Can you spot a
Duck, and a bat,
A blimp, a squid,
And three different hats,

A witch, a kite,
A pie in the sky
Three parachutes,
And a pig that can fly?

There's a boomerang,
A lost umbrella,
Six balloons, and
A purple propeller.

Can you spot a magnet, a CD, and TV,
A sailing ship, a house, and a chimpanzee,
A barrel, a bottle, and four star fish,
Five astronauts, and a satellite dish?
Find a golf ball, and a horse with wings,
A nut, a bolt, and planetary rings.

Can you spot an apple core,
A bunch of grapes, a soda can,
Corn on the cob, and two hot dogs,
A carrot, and a gingerbread man?

Can you find a pizza pie,
Three different types of cheese,
An avocado, half a tomato,
And four little honey bees?

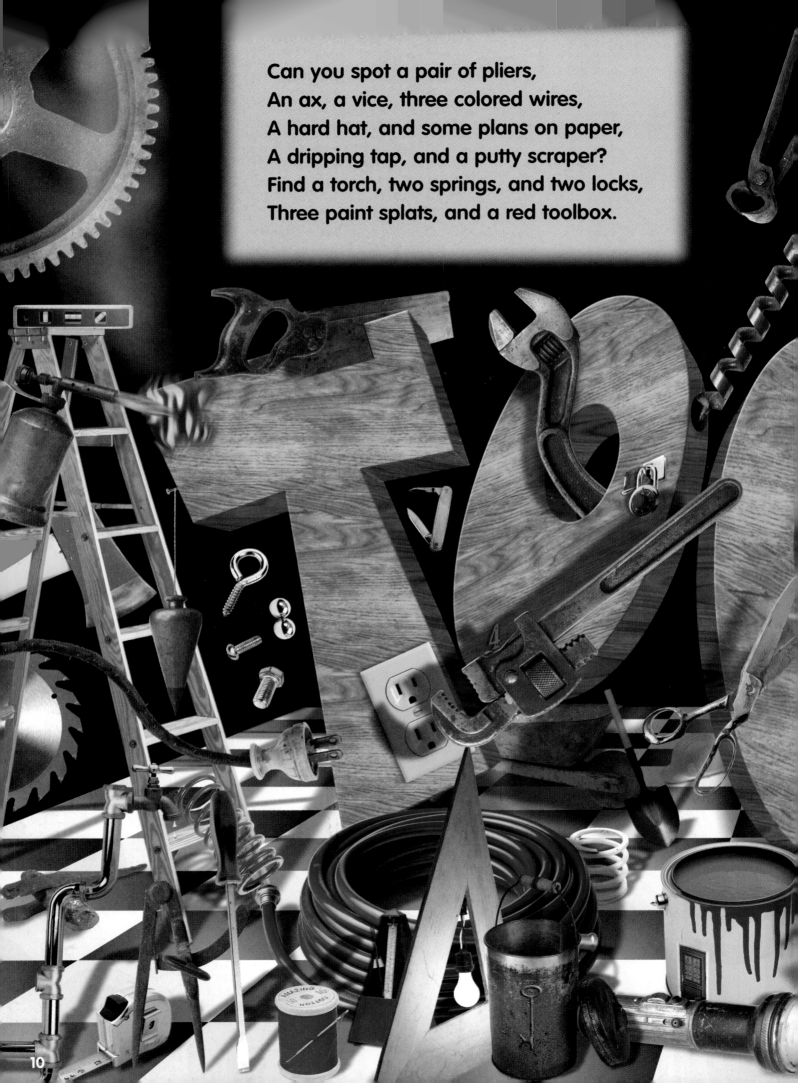

Can you spot a pair of pliers,
An ax, a vice, three colored wires,
A hard hat, and some plans on paper,
A dripping tap, and a putty scraper?
Find a torch, two springs, and two locks,
Three paint splats, and a red toolbox.

Can you spot a leopard,
A cow, two bulls, two seals,
Two stone cats, a welcome mat,
And three ferris wheels?

Can you find a baby bear,
A vintage car, a spear,
Five dinosaurs, a clock, a score,
A moose, a sheep, a deer?

AMAZING FALLS ->

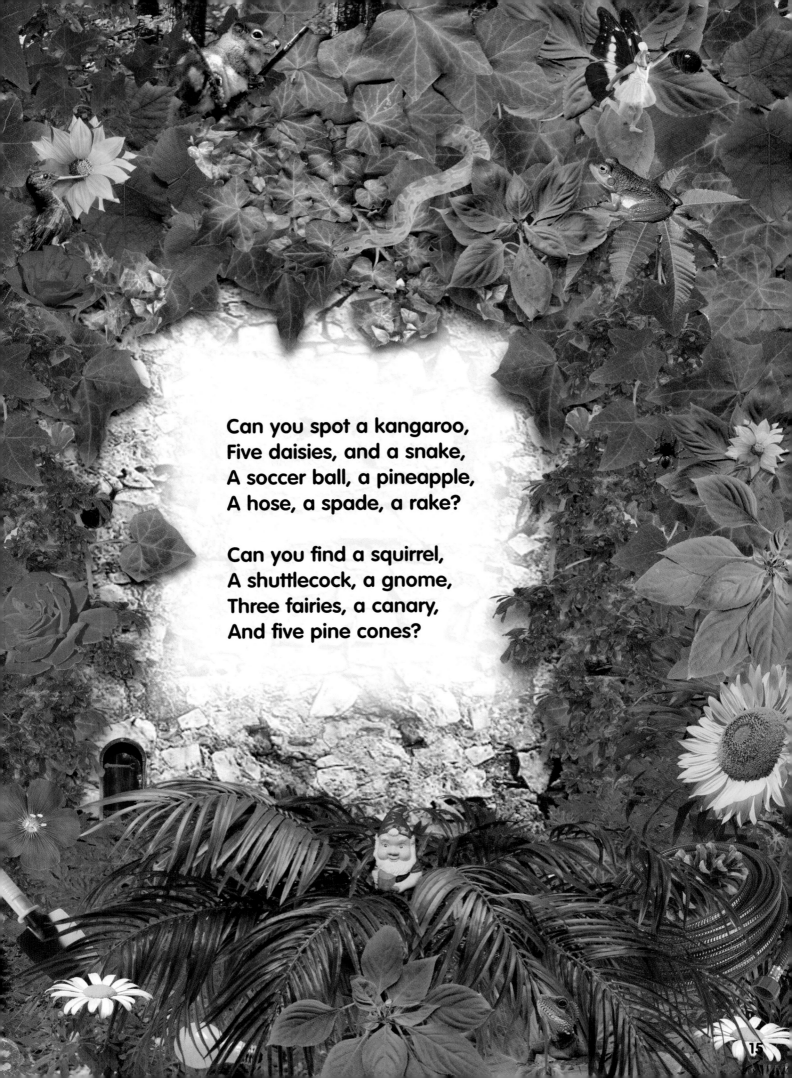

Can you spot a kangaroo,
Five daisies, and a snake,
A soccer ball, a pineapple,
A hose, a spade, a rake?

Can you find a squirrel,
A shuttlecock, a gnome,
Three fairies, a canary,
And five pine cones?

Can you spot a bird, and a pen,
A telephone, and ten past ten,
A truck, a puppet, two buckets, a tie,
A rabbit, a boot, and a butterfly?
Find a juke box, a feather, a star,
A whistle, a flipper, a drum, and guitar.

Can you spot a measuring tape,
And a bright red bus,
A computer, and the pyramids,
Three coins, an abacus?

Can you find nine rabbits,
Two sums that total seven,
A crane, a train, an hourglass,
Three sums that equal eleven?

Can you spot a set of keys,
And a red lipstick,
Seven coins, a pack of gum,
And a little candlestick?

Can you spot three brushes,
And a sticky first-aid strip,
Golden wings, five shiny rings,
And a tiny pair of lips?

Can you spot three dominos,
Two giraffes, and tic-tac-toe,
Three red dice, another blue,
A pawn, a knight, and a joker too?
Find eight jacks, a queen, a king,
Two darts, a clown, and a yo-yo string.

Can you spot a goldfish,
An apple, and cartoon,
A skier, wolf, and tomahawk,
A spider, and baboon?

Find a bear, a skunk, a poodle,
And a slide trombone,
A donkey, and a lobster,
A watch, and microphone.

Can you spot a pumpkin head,
Three balls, and a dragon,
Two lizards, and a wizard,
And a little red wagon?

Can you find a pair of gloves,
Two orange boots, and a frog,
A car, a train, a cowboy,
Three mice, two cats, four dogs?

POEM OF THE DAY

Fancy that,
A dancing cat,
To entertain the fans,

His only friend,
A singing hen,
Would clap if she had hands.

Benton Frappke December, 1908

AMAZING

See if you can spot these things in every picture:

Can you find the words "SPOT WHAT," A mermaid, and a four, A ladybug, a lightbulb, And a little blue door?

Juke Box

Blimp

Rules For The Spot What Amazing Game

1. Flip a coin, to see who goes first.
2. The winner of the coin toss chooses a picture from the book and then picks something for the other person to find, saying, for example, "Can you spot a pumpkin head?"
3. The spotter must then find the item.
4. If he or she can't spot it, the winner gets 5 points and shows him or her where it is.

5. Then the winner takes another turn and chooses an item for the other person to spot.
6. If the spotter can find the item, then he or she gets 5 points and now it's his or her turn.
7. The first to reach 30 points wins but you could also set your own limit of 50, or even 100 points.

You can also make the game more interesting by putting a time limit of one to three minutes on the search.

Solitaire Game

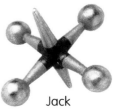

Jack

The Spot What Challenge

The following items are much harder to find, so get ready for the challenge.

Scraper

King

Flight
(page 4/5)

A butterfly
4 green leaves
3 hour glasses
An eagle
The world's first plane
A pair of socks
2 elastic bands

Food
(page 8/9)

3 balloons
3 chili peppers
Some teeth
A Christmas tree
6 flying peanuts
6 blue candles
6 strawberries

Cat

Space
(page 6/7)

All 12 zodiac symbols
A parking meter
A picnic
A space shuttle
4 telescopes
Venus and Mars
A kazoo

Tools
(page 10/11)

5 keys
A needle
3 cogs
3 measuring tools
3 different saws
A microscope
A metronome

Boomerang

Ferris Wheel

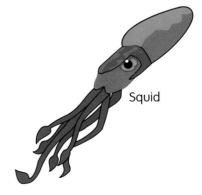
Squid

Tomahawk

Soda Can

Arena
(page 12/13)

7 jacks
5 barrels
An indian brave
A moon
4 shields
The words "GO GO DANCE"
A path to spell AMAZING

Blue
(page 16/17)

A typewriter
A seahorse
12 musical notes
5 fish
4 boats
4 balls
A rocking chair

Mermaid

Nature
(page 14/15)

A spider
An owl
A hungry bee
A nest
2 lizards
7 snails
A hummingbird

Numbers
(Page 18/19)

The word "APRIL"
2 boats
3 dominos
A barometer
4 playing cards
The word "RADAR"
The Sun

Metronome

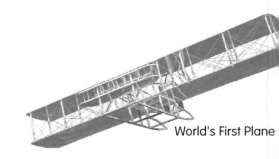
World's First Plane

Spade

Zodiac Symbol

Purse

(page 20/21)

5 diamonds
A frog
A cat
A pair of scissors
An umbrella
A ticket to Wonderland
A pen

Monitors

(page 24/25)

7 escaped butterflies
A potted plant
A rock band
A door handle
A jack
2 cameras
"CHANNEL 17"

Egg With Legs

Games

(page 22/23)

A fish bowl
A dog
4 flies
A thimble
Solitaire game
A pig
14 marbles

Bedroom

(page 26/27)

4 dinosaurs
23 yellow stars
An elephant
6 musical instruments
A fairy
A green plane
7 bears

Dog

Cowboy

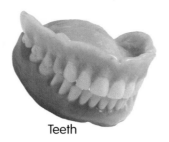
Teeth

Hourglass

Acknowledgements

We would like to thank the following people:

Albert Meli from Continuous Recall
Sam Grimmer
Peter Wakeman
Peter Tovey Studios
Samantha Boardman
Kelly-Anne Thompson
Kristie Maxwell
Kate Bryant
Heather Hammonds
Miles Summers
Little Ashlie, Michael, Nicole and James for lending their toys

Special thanks to Tsutomu Higo for the use of geometric models for 'Numbers'
www.asahi-net.or.jp/~nj2t-hg/

Furniture for "Bedroom" created by:
Christopher Peregrine Timms
www.christophertimms.com.au

Barometer

Diamond

Shuttlecock